Countries of the World

France

by Michael Dahl

Content Consultant:
Noah Cohrssen
National Services Coordinator
Alliance Française, National Office

Bridgestone Books
an imprint of Capstone Press

Bridgestone Books are published by Capstone Press
818 North Willow Street, Mankato, Minnesota 56001
http://www.capstone-press.com

Library of Congress Cataloging-in-Publication Data
Dahl, Michael S.
    France/by Michael Dahl.
    p. cm.--(Countries of the world)
    Includes bibliographical references and index.
    Summary: Tells the history and describes the landscape, people, animals, food, sports, and culture of the largest country in western Europe.
    ISBN 1-56065-737-5
    1. France--Juvenile literature. [1. France.] I. Title. II. Series. III. Series: Countries of the world (Mankato, Minn.)
DC29.3.D34   1998
944--dc21
                                   97-44466
                                     CIP
                                     AC

Editorial credits:
Editor, Christy Steele; cover design, Timothy Halldin; interior graphics, James Franklin;
  photo research, Michelle L. Norstad

Photo credits:
Brian Beck, 6
Jean S. Buldain, 8, 14
Capstone Press, 5 (left)
French Government Tourist Office, 10, 16; Dan Aubry, 20
International Stock/Chad Ehlers, cover
Richard Hamilton Smith, 18
Jean Daniel Sudres, 12
Unicorn Stock Photos/Marie Mills and David Cummings, 5 (right)

Table of Contents

Fast Facts

Name: Republic of France

Capital: Paris

Population: More than 58 million

Language: French

Religion: Mainly Roman Catholic

Size: 210,026 square miles (546,068 square kilometers)

France is about the size of the U.S. state of Texas.

Crops: Grains, corn, soybeans

Maps

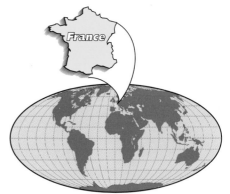

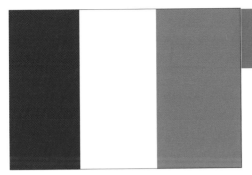

Flag

France's flag is called le tricolore. Tricolore means three colors in French. The left band is blue. The middle band is white. The right band is red. Red and blue once stood for the city of Paris. White stood for the king of France. The flag brought these colors together. This showed that the people of France were also joined together.

Currency

The unit of currency in France is the franc. The franc is divided into 100 centimes.

About 5.7 francs equal one U.S. dollar.

The Land of France

France is the largest country in western Europe. It is about the same size as the state of Texas. France has a six-sided shape. This is why French people sometimes call France the héxagon. A hexagon is a shape with six equal sides.

Two of Europe's major mountain ranges are in France. The Pyrenees (PEER-uh-neez) are in the south. They separate France from Spain. The Alps are in eastern France. They separate France from Germany, Switzerland, and Italy. The Alps are the highest mountains in Europe. People from around the world ski in France's mountains.

The Massif (mah-SEEF) Central takes up one-sixth of France. It is an area of high, flat land.

Two major bodies of water border France. The Atlantic Ocean is on the western coast of France. The Mediterranean Sea is on the southern coast of France.

Two of Europe's major mountain ranges are in France.

Life at Home

Most French people live in towns or cities. Their houses and apartments have large, open rooms. Children usually each have their own bedroom.

French people often meet their friends at cafés. A café is a small eating place. Some cafés serve food outdoors.

The kitchen is the center of the French home. French families eat most of their meals together. Eating is an important part of family life.

Sunday lunches are a tradition in France. A tradition is a practice continued for many years.

In the city, most families go to restaurants on Sunday. In the country, many families invite people to their homes. Sunday lunches can have several courses and last all afternoon.

French people often spend time with friends at cafés.

Going to School

Most French children attend school from age two to age 16. Children aged two to five go to maternelle. Maternelle is like nursery school in North America. At maternelle, children play games, learn songs, and paint.

Children attend ecole primaire from age five to age 10. Ecole primaire is like elementary school in North America. Children attend collège from age 11 to 14. This is like junior high school in North America. Next, children attend lycée. This is like a North American high school.

Many schools require students to wear uniforms. French schools have longer school days than other schools in Europe. The school day lasts from early morning to late afternoon.

Students sometimes take field trips to famous places in France. They learn about French history and art on field trips.

Students take field trips to famous places in France.

French Food

Food is important in France. There are more than 150 food societies in France. Members get together to enjoy their favorite foods.

Bread is an important part of most French meals. French people like different kinds of bread. They eat long loaves of crusty bread called baguettes (bah-GETZ). Croissants (kwah-SAHNTSS) are another popular form of bread. Croissants are light, flaky rolls.

French meals often include cheese and wine. French people make more than 400 kinds of cheese. French cheese and wine are sold around the world.

Some French cooks specialize in haute cuisine (OHT kwi-ZEEN). Haute cuisine means fancy, well-prepared food.

Parts of France are famous for special foods. For example, people in Burgundy prepare Burgundy beef.

Some French cooks specialize in haute cuisine.

Animals in France

Many kinds of animals live in France. Rabbits, foxes, and deer live in France's fields and forests. Some animals live mostly in the mountains. Small herds of ibex wander in the Alps. An ibex is a wild goat. Brown bears and boars also live in the mountains. A boar is a wild pig.

The Camargue (kuh-MARG) is an area of wetland in southern France. Flamingos and Egyptian vultures live there. Herds of wild bulls and horses travel through the area.

Several species are in danger of dying out in France. A species is a kind of animal. These species include badgers, otters, and beavers. The brown bear and lynx are also in danger. French people are trying to save these animals.

Wild bulls travel through the Camargue.

French Sports

More than half of the French people take part in sports. The most popular sports in France are soccer and skiing. Bicycling and tennis are also favorite sports.

The Tour de France is a famous bicycle race. The race lasts for several weeks. Bicyclists work in teams. They must pedal 2,500 miles (4,025 kilometers) over mountain roads and through towns.

People in France also enjoy water sports. They swim and water ski along France's beaches. The French Riviera (ri-vee-AIR-uh) is famous for its beaches. In France, the French Riviera is called Côte d'Azur (COHT duh-ZOOR).

Many French people enjoy playing petanque (puh-TONK). Players use small metal balls and a small wooden ball. They try to roll their metal balls close to the wooden ball.

Many French people enjoy playing petanque.

Paris

Paris is the capital of France. The Seine (SAYN) River flows through the middle of Paris. It divides Paris into the Left Bank and the Right Bank.

More than two million people live in Paris. This makes Paris Europe's most crowded capital.

Paris has many famous buildings. The Cathedral of Notre Dame (NOH-truh DAHM) is one of them. A cathedral is a large church. The cathedral of Notre Dame is decorated with gargoyles. Gargoyles are make-believe creatures made of stone.

The Eiffel (EYE-fil) Tower is France's most famous sight. It is 985 feet (296 meters) tall. People can see 50 miles (81 kilometers) from the top of the tower.

Paris also has famous museums. The Louvre (LOOV) is France's best-known museum. The Louvre displays many of the world's most famous paintings.

The Eiffel Tower is France's most famous sight.

Holidays

Many French holidays are the same as holidays in North America. Christmas is an important holiday in France. People in France observe Easter, too.

Many people celebrate Mardi Gras (MAR-dee GRAH) in March. Mardi Gras means fat tuesday in French. Mardi Gras is the day before Lent. Lent is the 40 days before Easter. People eat crabs and wear costumes during Mardi Gras. Some even march in parades.

French people celebrate Bastille (bas-TEEL) Day every July 14. Cities set off fireworks. People attend outdoor dances and parties.

In the past, the Bastille was a prison. French people stormed the Bastille on July 14, 1789. This was an important event during the French Revolution. Today, the Bastille is an opera house. An opera is a play in which actors sing the words.

Many people celebrate Mardi Gras in March.

Hands On: Play Petanque

Many French people enjoy playing petanque. You can play petanque with your friends.

What You Need

Three tennis balls for each player
One softball

What You Do

1. Ask each player to initial three tennis balls.
2. Choose a starting line. Ask one player to stand behind the line. Ask the player to throw the softball in any direction. Players must be able to see the softball from the starting line.
3. Have the first player throw his or her tennis balls toward the softball.
4. Have the other players throw their tennis balls at the softball. The players must stand behind the starting line to throw.
5. Check to see whose tennis ball is closest to the softball. The person who throws a tennis ball closest to the softball receives one point. Whoever gets five points first is the winner.

Learn to Speak French

good	bon	(BOHN)
good-bye	au revoir	(OH ruh-VWAH)
good morning	bonjour	(bohn-JOOR)
or **good day**		
great	grand	(GRAHN)
no	non	(NOH)
please	s'il vous plaît	(SEE VOO PLAY)
sorry	désolé	(day-zoh-LAY)
thank you	merci	(mare-SEE)
yes	oui	(WEE)

Words to Know

boar (BOR)—a wild pig

café (kaf-AY)—a small eating place

cathedral (kuh-THEE-druhl)—a large church

gargoyle (GAR-goil)—a make-believe creature made of stone

ibex (EYE-bex)—a wild goat

Mardi Gras (MAR-dee GRAH)—the day before Lent

species (SPEE-sheez)—a kind of animal

Read More

Dunford, Mick. *France.* New York: Thomson Learning, 1995.

Sturges, Jo. *Discovering France.* New York: Crestwood House, 1993.

Useful Addresses and Internet Sites

Française National Office
2819 Ordway Street NW
Washington, DC 20008

Embassy of France
4101 Reservoir Road NW
Washington, DC 20007

Excite Travel: France
http://www.city.net/countries/france/

French Embassy in Washington, D.C.
http://www.info-france-usa.org

Index